BIZARRE ARCHITECTURE

BIZARRE ARCHITECTURE

CHARLES JENCKS

All photographs by C.A. Jencks unless otherwise noted.

Back cover

RICARDO BOFILL and ATELIER, *Walden Seven*, Barcelona, 1974-6. The obsessive repetition of cylindrical balconies, stepped shapes and red tile on a massive dwelling block. Note the gigantic front door and the twelve storey cut-out holes that allow light, and wind, to penetrate into the courtyards. The planning of the apartments is as ingenious in its geometrical sophistication as the exterior. In the background can be seen the concrete factory which Bofill converted into his studio, and Architects' Dream, replete with hanging gardens and cypresses.

Published in the United States of America in 1979 by
RIZZOLI INTERNATIONAL PUBLICATIONS, INC.
712 Fifth Avenue/New York 10019

Library of Congress Catalog Card Number: 78-68916
ISBN: 0-8478-0222-1

Printed and bound in Hong Kong

CONTENTS

Figures refer to illustration numbers

INTRODUCTION

'In a venerable Chinese encyclopedia "animals are divided into: a) belonging to the Emperor, b) embalmed, c) tame, d) sucking pigs, e) sirens, f) fabulous, g) stray dogs, h) included in the present classification, i) frenzied, j) innumerable, k) drawn with a very fine camel-hair brush, 1) et cetera, m) having just broken the water pitcher, n) that from a long way off look like flies"'.
(Quoted from a telephone call with Demetri Porphyrios who was in turn quoting an English translation of Michel Foucault's translation of Borges' quote in Spanish, whose original source is hard to discover.)

Bizarre architecture is hard to think about. Like the capricious classification of animals above, it falls between habitual categories of thought and seems lost in a mist of scarcely traceable sources. Bizarre architecture, if it is being properly bizarre, defies the well-carved pidgeonhole, for the obvious reason that bizarre means unconventional and unlikely. If you can place a bizarre building in a classification system, as you must in order to perceive it, then it immediately loses some of its magical property. This is the quandry and challenge for this book, as it was for the previous one in this field, *Fantastic Architecture*, and as it is for anyone confronted with an eccentric or fabulous building for the first time. How are we to appreciate the unclassifiable without domesticating it?

There are various paths we can follow which don't predict an outcome, or at least an habitual response. Bizarre architecture, when first seen, is rather like a Rorschak test which calls forth certain non-standard images. An unusual building, the Sydney Opera House, was originally perceived as 'fish swallowing each other' and 'a scrum of nuns' among many other images (see plate 51). No doubt these meanings relate both to certain formal aspects of the building *and* to the preoccupations of the viewer: those who do not play rugby might not see the white 'sails' as a nun's cowls and thus not perceive their clash this way. Rather the confrontation of white shapes might be 'a traffic accident — with no survivors'.

For those who are otherwise disposed it might be a more harmonious and organic metaphor: 'opening petals of a white flower' or 'shells erupting on a beach'. According to the journalistic cliché the billowing forms were like the 'white sails in Sydney Harbour'. However, for the architect these forms were like orange peels, the spume of waves and the wing of an eagle photographed in flight. Whatever metaphor we choose as most apt, an important point emerges which distinguishes this building from normal architecture: it is outside the class of opera houses, indeed of all previous building. It seeks to be one of a kind, unclassifiable, like Alfred Jarry's impossible but desirable 'pataphysics', the science of singular events. As soon as there are two, similiar Sydney Opera houses it ceases to be bizarre, and becomes instead

PHILIP JOHNSON, *The Garden Grove Community Church,* 1977 (under construction). Designed, as so many churches this century, as a glass crystal which illuminates the congregation with its rays of Divine Geometry and a face known as Crystallology. (Louis Checkman)

conventional. From this conclusion further points may be supposed: the designer of an extraordinary building may want an impossible thing. He may wish his work to remain extraordinary and at the same time want it to be accepted as a significant contribution to architectural history. Such a contradiction does, I believe, lie in the heart of almost every architect treated in this book. Antonio Gaudí, Erich Mendelsohn and Frank Lloyd Wright, to name three, were perfectly well aware that they were producing outrageous buildings but they hoped that with time and understanding these creations would be accepted as perfectly valid extensions of tradition — as they have, partly, been. With acceptance and copying, however, goes a certain price. Their buildings are no longer perceived as so extraordinary and outrageous; they become examples of 'Organic architecture' or 'Expressionism', that is an art-historical pidgeonhole. Perhaps the point of a book on Bizarre architecture is to give back to these buildings their original sense of curiosity? We should invent new categories, like those of the Chinese encyclopedia, which are as unlikely and non-parallel and disjunctive and ungrammatical as the buildings originally were.

On the other hand, we might adopt a straightforward descriptive approach. This is the conventional way to treat outrageous and baroque architecture — as if it were normal classical building which just happened to have funny things going on. Most histories of Baroque architecture are written as dead-pan accounts with masses of historical fact and iconological analysis surrounding the object of investigation, as if this were appropriate[1]. Henry-Russell Hitchcock's *Rococo Architecture in Southern Germany,* 1968, is an extreme example of this genre where one is told almost everything about these extraordinary buildings except how singular and moving they are. The supposition is that the reader can supply the missing feeling and that all he needs are the facts. *Dream Palaces (Les Palais du Rêve)* by Claude Arthaud is another investigation into historical buildings of the unlikely, but it also proceeds by assuming that we want to domesticate the unusual and package it according to habitual categories.

One of the few works that begins to approach the chaos with a discontinuous set of classifiers is *Fantastic Architecture*, by the German authors Ulrich Conrads and Hans G. Sperlich[2]. Here we have a glimpse of the abundant and riotous universe underlying the bizarre, where thought itself follows the plurality of motives which make a building different in the first place. Merely to list their subchapters and categories gives an idea of the richness and singularity which is at stake. Architecture is discussed as: 'found object, extreme tangibility, fantastic frameworks, fascination with the transparent, sheltering cave, labyrinth and spiral, formally restricted improvisations, pre-figured architecture, hovering architecture, architectural utopia, Futurist city, obsession with height, utopian cliques, "Utopian Letters", Utopia today'. There is none of the tidy-mindedness usual to the genre of architectural history. Indeed we wouldn't be surprised to find in this list, 'g) stray dogs', 'i) frenzied' or 'n) that from a long way off looks like flies'. Classification may be on a single motif, or one idea which is exaggerated, a singular occurrence.

What is of course impossible is not to classify, for we look at things through categories not with uneducated eyes[3]. And these categories of seeing are above all historical and at the same time personal. Thus periods of architecture are labelled Mannerist and Baroque and we seek to find in this work the very qualities we have pre-assumed in our categories. Since Baroque originally meant 'bizarre' among other things and the architecture was damned as such, we can approach this category with an expectant, ironical relish. Because the term bároque changed from being an abusive epithet into a neutral, classificatory term we can see this irony in trying to run history backwards and recapture the original *'bizarre'* — if that is our intention. We could argue that it is historically inaccurate not to be shocked by Borromini's 'strange and capricious' towers, Guarini's impossible, 'Gothic-like' domes and so forth. Our search then becomes one to find suitable words, metaphors and categories which can give back to bizarre architecture the surprise and shock it has lost through domestication. Perhaps like youth this can never be recaptured. After all, once we learn that a grotesque or gargoyle doesn't bite it is hard to imagine that it does. But the search for Bizarre architecture must be conducted as if this were possible, as an exploration into an unchartered territory where the map is invented while proceeding; otherwise all that is discovered is the same old Normal architecture, but with kinks.

One of the bizarre experiences of living today is, as Marshall McLuhan has pointed out, reading the mixed salad that is a daily newspaper. The juxtaposition of Brehznev and abortion, or the Theory of Black Holes and Miss World, is surprising if not ludicrous. Just as we are reading about the Middle East peace settlement our eye is caught by a piece about how the Japanese are manufacturing a killer whale to frighten off dolphins — a kind of automated Jaws with multitrack stereo screams. These stories have, of course, nothing to do with each other except their fortuitous encounter cheek-by-jowl in adjoining columns of print. But the continual presence of such juxtapositions in the newspaper, or the city street, develops a taste for extreme contrasts and incongruity. The Surrealists made this into a principle of art ('Beauty is the fortuitous encounter of an umbrella and a sewing machine on a dissecting table', a nineteenth century definition they liked to quote). And they invented the game of 'Exquisite Corpse', that pastime whereby several people construct a figure by drawing parts, in hidden folds of a paper, until a hybrid monster is created. There is a type of twentieth century architecture which is equally hybrid, and sometimes monstrous. For instance Antonio Gaudí combined images of bones, sculls, seaweed, lava, clowns, sequins, fish and dragon in his famous 'House of Bones' built in Barcelona, 1905-7 (plate 1). There is an interpretation which ties all these images together (see caption), but nonetheless their juxtaposition is bizarre. This our first category, 'Bizarre Juxtaposition', varies from such opposition of images to the opposition of styles, content and building material. We have distinguished the last aspect as yet another category, 'Ad hoc juxtaposition', but clearly there are more distinctions to be made and they might not have to sound so academic and abstract. For instance the 'House in the Clouds' (2) which juxtaposes a pitched-roof house with a knife-like chimney and a clapboard tower base might just as well be called a member of that large and delirious class — 'Disguised-Water-Tower', since that's what it is.

Several examples of Bizarre Juxtaposition are the result of that turn of the century eclecticism which grew out of the Queen Anne Revival — Olbrich's buildings at Darmstadt (3), John Hudson Thomas' and Bernard Maybeck's work in San Francisco (4,5) and the extreme incongruities of Chinatown and Chevron Gas added onto a nineteenth century apartment building (6). This category becomes quite delirious when commercialised, either by banks, department stores, Walt Disney or the environmental team known as S.I.T.E. (7-9, 15, 16). This team, led by the sculptor James Wines, juxtaposes simple department stores, or large commercial packing crates, with all sorts of images including a waving parking lot, a sliding wall (15) and a crumbling wall (16) to produce the architectural equivalent of a 'one-liner' (a joke one punch-line long). The pre-eminent virtue of this work is to provide humour for a building type which has never intentionally had it before — the minimum commercial box or shed. On one level it's a natural evolution of the bill-board into the building, so that a single zany idea captures the eye to advertise the product while, at the same time, cheap and boring space is still maximized. Robert Venturi has designed several of these 'building-boards', one of which has been influenced by S.I.T.E. (64); but James Wines has pushed the formula in a much more lyrical direction.

If the results have an obvious fault they share it with advertisement and one-liners in general: no matter how good (or good/bad) the joke, it's over in a flash. In fact a whole category of commercial bizarre — 'Delirious Trademark' (61-64) — suffers from this shortness of breath. The buildings in the shape of hot-dogs, brown derbys, big donuts, pianos, or dinosaurs (50), that is iconic buildings, can be too quickly dismissed because of their obviousness. A literal representation of some idea has the potential drawback that it only represents the obvious idea. On the other hand, a richness might be provided by the surrounding context, or a transformation of the idea on further levels. Thus the anthropomorphism of Rudolph Steiner's work at Dornach is extended to zoomorphism and symbolism concerning natural growth (46, 47). The basic idea that the body should be represented in a building is played with explicitly and implicitly. We are thus never quite sure whether we are looking at a face or monster, tree or cosmic diagram. The meanings are allowed to intermingle with a literal fluidity, the undulating concrete.

As can be seen from the foregoing discussion, categories of the bizarre *are* permissive and polymorphous; already we've jumped over several classes of this book in order to see further, implicit classes. We could generalize this aspect as 'the case for an illegitimate architecture', the case for miscegenation and architectural bastards. I've discussed this aspect in *Daydream Houses of Los Angeles* and I hope to show its existence in bizarre historical buildings, *Exotic Architecture*, because it is one of the most misunderstood qualities of the whole genre. We are used to applauding works which are pure, which have a clear paternity, whether International Style or Classical. When confronted with a building which has two or more bloodlines we tend to regard it as uncertain or mixed up. Thus whole classes of building are disregarded, or considered of inferior breeding: those between Renaissance and Mannerism for instance. A lot of English and German architecture from 1530 to 1630 falls into this non-category, one I would call 'Mannersance' except that this ugly label might further the opprobrium. The point is, however, that hybrid building often seeks to be hybrid and we misjudge it by applying the canons of stylistic purity. The old design definition of a camel — 'a horse put together by a committee' — not only brings out the usual distaste for hybrids but also the latent fact that a camel isn't a bad animal trying to be a good horse and failing, but a perfectly valid, ugly, splendid quadruped in its own right. In like manner much Bizarre Juxtaposition knows it is hybrid and ugly, but it is trying to be so much else as well: humorous, rich in associations and striking. Basically it says with so much other romantic art, 'I'd rather be interesting than good, I prefer character to beauty'. We may disagree with the goal, but at least should try not to misunderstand it. Goodhardt-Rendel said of the Queen Anne Revival that it was 'a Gothic game played with neo-classical counters' and he may have regretted the fact; but he did acknowledge that the Queen Anne wasn't trying to be either Gothic or Neo-Classical and getting it wrong.

'Adhoc Juxtaposition', the second category of the unlikely, is almost the same as the first in its interest with contrast, humour and using parts in a new context. In fact we might just as well have labelled this class 'etcetera' after our Chinese encyclopedia, to indicate that it carries on the first class with minor differences. These concern the use of pre-existing parts — pebbles, stones, broken glass and china, wire-mesh, glass cullet and hard coal (in Bruce Goff's case, 18,19), caravans, scrapmetal, trees that have been blown down in a hurricane, and a whole assortment of things floatable, which make up the boathouse community at Sausalito (20,21).

The enjoyment of building with left-overs is clear in all those examples. There may be an economic or utilitarian argument involved as well, but basically these architects, or amateurs, get pleasure from showing their discoveries left in the raw. Thus with the French postman Ferdinand Cheval or the Italian immigrant to Los Angeles, Simon Rodia, one is ultra-conscious of pebbles, or bottles (12-14). In both cases their previous identity is emphasised, the fact that they enjoyed an autonomous existence apart from the present context. All Adhocism, or the collage of pre-existing systems, shows this autonomy of parts. Whereas eclecticism merges styles and materials to form a whole statement, Adhocism emphasizes the parts and their previous contexts. While eclecticism may try to put Humpty-Dumpty back together again, Adhocism follows all the king's horses and all the king's men. The results are bizarre then not only for their juxtaposition, but because the part, the detail, may take over and distort one's perception of the whole. At the two crumbling buildings for instance (16,17) we are more likely to focus in on the crumble than to look at the whole, which in any case is rather boring. This aspect of substitution, of *pars pro toto*, is characteristic of much bizarre architecture which fetishizes certain details such as the corner joint or roof.

Our next set of categories is just as slippery as the first two, and like them could be regrouped under different headings depending on what aspects we find pertinent. Since the bizarre is by definition non-conventional there is bound to be objection to the classes I propose, although perhaps less so here: 'Fantasy Eclecticism' is a fairly well-established genre stemming from the nineteenth century, the Brighton Pavilion and the confections of Ludwig II, the fantasy king of Bavaria. In this century the tradition has been carried on with Randolph Hearst's eclecticism at San Simeon, Sid Grauman's Chinese Theatre in Hollywood (22), Communist revivals in Stalinist Baroque (24,25) and many commercial buildings which inject an eclectic element into a prosaic building type in order to startle the passer-by into entering them, or else aid the consumer in his particular fantasy (26-28). The Japanese Love-hotel in the form of Cinderella's castle at Disneyland, which mimicked Ludwig II's castle in Bavaria, which copied the Duc de Berry's fantasies in France is a good example of this genre (29). It is a copy of a pastiche of a replica of a fantasy which might not even have existed in the first place — the Duc de Berry's castles come down to us only in the exquisite paintings of *Les Très Riches Heures*. These are fairytale castles with beautiful white turrets and blue slate roofs, the essence of a picturesque castle with its pertinent elements exaggerated to confirm one idea of what a castle is about — security, power, beauty and 'a place high in the clouds'.

Fantasies can obviously come in a myriad of forms, but for architects in this century there are particularly two areas that have exerted a strong fascination: the technological and geometric. These again have roots in the nineteenth century as indeed in ancient architecture, with the vast waterworks, aqueducts and bridges of the Romans, and the geometrical obsessions of the Egyptians and Renaissance architects. The two categories are the very essence of 'architects' architecture', which is not to say that the public doesn't also share in this fascination, and enjoy the genre. Rather we could say that only architects get deeply involved in the intricacies of the play involved: they follow the moves closely the way chess enthusiasts play through the games of the Old Masters. Why, if technology and geometry are the very stuff of architecture, do we term these categories bizarre? Because in the example shown these elements, or parts, have once again taken over control of the whole building and become an obsession, or fetish. I say this without meaning to condemn fetishism in general since, I believe, it can be shown that all good architecture highlights certain themes to the point of obsession, so that they dominate every aspect. Drama and art are based on this over-accentuation; redundancy is a keynote of rhetoric.

In the nineteenth century, the world expositions in London and Paris promoted 'Technological Fantasy' as a category of building and in this century the World Fair has played the same role. Then it was the Crystal Palace and Eiffel Tower, whereas today it is a giant inflatable in the shape of a fried egg (USA Pavilion), or elephant's bum (Fuji Pavilion, both Osaka 1970). Needless to say these bizarre metaphors were not intended by their authors but, quite as obviously, some untypical image was sought. With the Festival Plaza at Expo 70 there was a quite conscious intention to symbolise technology as a liberating fantasy. The giant space frame had various capsule units 'plugged-into' its skeleton, some of which could move about, and Arata Isozaki designed a series of movable, giant Robots (with the mandatory bug-eyes and flexing arms) that could putter about flashing lights in the best Sci-Fi tradition (30). Personally I find this fantasy more convincing when it is least expected, that is outside of a World's Fair, so I have chosen examples within an everyday or urban context: the apartment building made to look as if it were stacked caravan bodies, and with various exhaust pipes like a dragster; the Pompidou Centre in Paris, that meccano-set with its boney arms and pin joints; the movable building, the truck or bus, shaped like a cottage in thatch or a Gothic Church (32-7). In each case the technology is bizarre because of its juxtaposition, either with the surroundings or the function, thus making this category similar to our first one.

Geometrical Fantasy fetishizes the constructional detail, structural shape or spatial order, and sometimes in the case of Frank Lloyd Wright all three (38). His Beth Shalom Synagogue multiplies hexagonal and triangular shapes throughout plan, elevation and detail as if the congregation might otherwise forget the underlying symbol of their faith. Many churches today are following this crystal symbolism which was worked out in the early part of the century. Bruce Goff, Philip Johnson, even a large architectural office such as Skidmore, Owings and Merrill, have adapted the convention that faith is an explosion of light, or 'God is in the Crystals'. Given the search for a natural symbolism, one can see the logic of the metaphor. And of course it is comparable to the Gothic belief that geometry and light were two ultimate properties by which the Divine revealed His presence and instructed the faithful. What makes it bizarre today is the singularity with which it is done. When Philip Johnson finishes his Tower of Hope, or Crystal Cathedral, two miles from Disneyland, wider and higher than Notre Dame, accommodating four thousand worshippers and more in the parking lot, then one will know — because of the metaphors issuing from *Time, Newsweek* and the colour supplements — that Crystalosophy has finally gone public (see illustration).

Architects' geometry can often induce a kind of optical trance, or visual hypnotism, especially if the vectors of motion are picked out in colour. Paolo Portoghesi does this with coloured stripes in his Roman Casa Papanice. The vertical stripes on the exterior zip around in various rhythmical beats — actually the building was 'composed' according to a Vivaldi piece and other staccato melodies (40). The glisten of the glazed tile and the sparkling lightness of the whites and blues make the geometrical repetitions all the more dazzling. On the interior the geometry goes horizontal to create the visual equivalent of a whirly-gig, or a fairground spin-top. Walls ripple and zoom around corners, horizontal bands swing through ninety degree turns like Fangio at Le Mans, tubes of light telescope down from above into a pool of concentric ripples (41). If that last sounds like a mixed-up mixed metaphor then my only defence is to plead that Bizarre architecture induces this kind of hyperbole and piling up of imagery. Indeed the Baroque architect who Portoghesi has brilliantly analysed, Francesco Borromini, piles up one structural system, and metaphor, on top of another to produce the most bizarre church towers we know[4].

Geometrical tricks can often be played most effectively in a normal context. Peter Eisenman has shown in his eleven variations on the International Style house that prosaic motifs can be recharged with abnormal attributes. His houses, numbered 1-11 as if they were musical variations on the same theme, play with the right angle, flat white wall, white column and gridded window. It doesn't sound bizarre, or even different from Le Corbusier, but it is. Partly because the exterior syntax is reduced to white geometric shapes which, through an homogeneous treatment in colour and form, equate elements that are different (42). A column turns into a wall, gets bigger and turns into beam-window. Thus three elements which are usually distinguished in material and function become the same, and we perceive this equation as very bizarre indeed. The abnormality is underscored by carefully smashing the two right-angled geometries through each other, and working out the discordant collisions with a ruthless consistency (43). Perhaps only other architects, with explanatory diagrams in hand, can follow the full subtlety of this Chess Master and all the complicated forms of his self-check-mate, but everyone can respond to the sensuality and nonsense of the whole.

The remaining categories of the bizarre are more representational than Eisenman's abstract games. In one way or another they all call up precise images or refer to non-architectural things we know: animals, plants, the human body or such tangible things as donuts and shoes. This general type of architecture is called iconic because there is *some* connection between shape and idea, form and function, volume and traditional pattern. As in onomatopoeia where the sound is an echo to the sense (i.e. cuckoo, bang), the form is an echo to the content. This echoing can occur at a very abstract level as in Mendelsohn's and Steiner's work where dynamism is represented (44-7). Or the cues can be multiplied and made specific until one sees the whole whale and nothing but the whale (48). Between these extremes of iconicity the representational building oscillates, always in danger of becoming too abstract so that the message is lost, or too concrete, where there is only one message. The best of the genre thus mixes up the two extremes, giving some cues which are highly specific in order to heighten the perception of those which are hidden. Rudolph Steiner, for instance, makes use of anthropomorphic images for his Anthroposophical buildings (46, 47, 54). We approach the Goetheanum aware that it is some kind of face; perhaps that of a horse-shoe crab or the helmeted visage of a German sten-gunner (46). There are eyes, nose and hair, more or less where they should be, and as usual in this sort of building, a mouth-door. But the eyebrows are all over the place and shoulders have merged with the head and besides the whole thing is a lumpy turtle anyway, mixed in concrete. Just as we are trying to decide between these two types of ambiguity, seven more raise their ugly heads to mock our simple-minded explanations. This concrete lump is a pill-box and baroque facade, silver-grey dome and free-form sculpture, opening plant and bristling cactus and frozen custard. What these metaphors have in common is not much, except an organic quality. The general theme of living matter seems to run through the inert concrete calling out for anthropomorphic metaphors, yet denying any particular one.

For this general area of architectural representation I will coin the suitably bizarre epithet 'animalorphic'. As it sounds the word relates to anthropomorphic (man-like) and zoomorphic (animal-like) and Orphic (the mysteries and music of Orpheus) and animal (self-evident). Any more questions? Animalorphic architecture is obviously then a mixed architectural metaphor where body and vegetative images cohabit. As such it's a rather cannibalistic genre swallowing the categories such as Expressionism, the Einstein Tower (44), zoomorphic buildings, Saarinen's Whale at Yale (49), the Sydney Opera House and all its fish (51) and that very personable class of buildings Face Houses (52-60).

The Face House, or more generally, anthropomorphic building, has quite recently come into its own with a vast body of scholarly literature and a *bona fide* pedigree[5] ; Yale professors, Messrs Vincent Scully, George Hersey, Kent C. Bloomer and Charles Moore, have reputedly fallen off the lecture platform while extolling its virtue; an impressive battery of psychological armament is brought into play known as 'Body-Image Theory'; the examples of Vitruvius, Alberti, Palladio and of course Le Corbusier, are put forward to justify the genre; empathy and the 'pathetic fallacy' clinch the argument. A house must now 'rise up from the ground' on its legs, reveal its dynamic musculature, bat its window-eyes, wear its heart (chimney-hearth) on its sleeve (pitched roof), and hide its nether regions (furnace-stomach). And it must do all this implicitly, without the owner knowing. Any house which doesn't smile and talk back to the owner is alienated. A house without a centre is heartless; a flat-top abode is head-less; a Miesian glass box is deaf, dumb, blind and probably ought to be put out of its misery with dynamite. This is 'Body-Image Theory', or something like it. The serious part of the argument concerns the fact that people naturally have empathy with buildings, more particularly their own home, and that they quite unselfconsciously project bodily states, and physiognomic categories, onto built form. They speak about an 'up and down', 'back and front', 'head and heart' of an inanimate structure. In short they commit the pathetic fallacy — and in more ways than the linguistic. Sociologists have shown that in describing their homes people often confuse the architecture with their own life; psychological studies have shown that people identify the structure and symmetry of a building with their body. All this has led to quite conscious architectural animalorphism.

Antonio Gaudí and Bruce Goff (1,53,60) have stressed its humorous side, and when they put playful helmets or bug-eyes in their buildings one can be sure they were meant to entertain. J. M. Olbrich and Rudolph Steiner are perhaps more serious, at least heavy, with their faces (52,54) but they do, at the same time, bear resemblance to the comic-strip face houses in 'Wee Willie Winkle' which used to talk back to this character. The Face appears with amazing regularity in California bungalows, with their pitched-roof aedicules looking out at the street like father and son, and it is a common image in popular, and vernacular building (55).

It would be appropriate to end this survey of the bizarre with the category 'etcetera' to underline the plurality of types and the fact that only a few are shown here, but instead we finish with that hallucinatory type created by commerce, with help from the Surrealists, known as Delirious Trademark (61-4). This is another kind of representational building where the connection of form and content is delirious either because of its size (the Big Donut Drive-in sells big donuts but not *that* big) or contrast (The Donut Hole, which you drive a vehicle through, does not even sell edible round pieces of dough — it's a car wash). (62-63).

* * *

This excursion into unchartable territory has not adopted an historical approach, nor has it covered the entire field, nor illustrated many of the well-known examples (because they are known), but it has shown the variety of species, their peculiar heterogeneity, and an aspect which is not immediately obvious, nor granted immediate assent: that is bizarre building can really be quite good architecture. Too often it is dismissed at a glance or consigned to a lower level of critical repute somewhere in the basement along with doggeral and farce. While much of it is inconsequential, some of it produced by serious architects — Gaudí, Venturi, Mendelsohn, Eisenman, Utzon, Portoghesi — can reach the highest expressive level of the art. Indeed, generalizing out from this survey we might conclude that in any great building, the pyramids, the Parthenon, the churches of Borromini, there is always an obsession with some element or motif which makes these works, whatever else they may be, also bizarre.

1 Henry-Russell Hitchcock, *Rococo Architecture in Southern Germany*, Phaidon, London 1968; Claude Arthaud, *Les Palais du Rêve*, Paris-Match, Paris 1970.

2 Ulrich Conrads and Hans G. Sperlich, *Fantastic Architecture*, The Architectural Press, London 1963, originally published in German by Verlag GerdJatje, Stuttgart, 1960.

3 See E. H. Gombrich 'Classification and its Discontents' in *Norm and Form*, Phaidon Press, London, 1960, pp. 81-3

4 Paolo Portoghesi, *Borromini*, London and Cambridge, Mass., 1968.

5 Besides my own writing on the subject *(The Language of Post-Modern Architecture*, Academy, London, 1978, pp. 112-117) which gives some of the references including Carl Jung, there is Kent C. Bloomer and Charles W. Moore, *Body, Memory and Architecture,* Yale University Press, 1977; George Hersey *Pythagorean Palaces, Magic and Architecture in the Italian Renaissance,* Cornell University Press, Ithaca, 1976 and *High Victorian Gothic, A Study in Associationism,* The Johns Hopkins University Press, Baltimore, 1972. Vincent Scully's lectures and books stress the empathetic perception of architecture and implicit body metaphors which he finds.

1 ANTONIO GAUDI, *Casa Batlló*, Barcelona, 1904-6. The juxtaposition of images was made to signify a separatist wish: the dragon, Spain, is slayed by the Christian cross and sword of Barcelona's patron, Saint George, while below the sculls and bones of martyrs can be seen in the balconies and structure. In the background a procession of helmeted clowns can be seen, while the tiled front sparkles and modulates like the Mediterranean.

2 GLENNIE and WILSON, *House in the Clouds*, Thorpeness, Suffolk, 1925. A disguised water tank for this new, artificial village, juxtaposes colour, form and content. The idea of every pitched roof home having its chimney takes on a ludicrous power here. The proportions and transitions of the juxtaposed elements are well worked out and so play down the inherent

3 JOSEF-MARIA OLBRICH, *Artists Colony*, Darmstadt, 1889-1907. One of the great set-pieces of eclecticism combining i
one area the close juxtaposition of five or six styles (Art Nouveau, Vernacular, Proto-Modern, Stripped Classicism and, t
he right, Russian Orthodox Church design). The Wedding Tower, with its five 'fingers', nautical ornamental detail, phalli
hape and asymmetries becomes the focus of this sensitive and bizarre urban group.

4 JOHN HUDSON THOMAS, *Locke House*, Oakland, California, 1911. Stylistic juxtaposition mixes Queen Anne tower ar
verandah, Gothic buttresses, Mission Revival rough cast stucco, Arts and Crafts interiors, Italian arcades, Secessionist ornamen
The exaggeration of scale, the pronounced irregularity of profile, increase the feeling of oddness while the homogeneo

5 BERNARD MAYBECK, *Christian Science Church*, side entrance, Berkeley, 1910. Maybeck's finest building is a subtle clash of East and West, Japanese roofs and gates with Bay Area wood architecture and the Gothic. Romanesque piers are cast, along with their ornamental capitals, in concrete while other touches – a curtain wall, and asbestos siding – are Modern. Maybeck's gigantic Flamboyant tracery provides a sensuous sign of sacred entry.

Wild Enough, Franklin Street, San Francisco. The Queen Annish apartment block in greenish copper is painted ad for Marine World, circa 1970, and a Chevron Gas Station in the Late-Late Ming-Ming Style in Chinatown). In deep focus the juxtaposition gets even more disturbing as a Hughes aircraft takes off — the West'.

7 WALT DISNEY AND IMAGINEERS, *Disneyland*, Anaheim, 1955 +. The poop deck of Casey Jones rubs bottoms with a railroad charabanc and fibreglass Matterhorn, which a mountain climber climbs every hour on the hour. Bizarre juxtaposition is the major compositional method of amusement parks, and because it is expected it's less bizarre than it might be. The seven types of circulation including submarine travel are, however, surprisingly nutty.

ANON, *Security State Bank,* Wisconsin, c. 1971? One has to congratulate this firm which specializes in zany banking juxta
osition, because they'll tack on a classical pediment to anything, even as here a mobile home (how's that for 'security'
dvertisement. Surrealism, conventional signification, all taken to ludicrous extremes produce this beautiful mad encounte

e City, c. 1975? One way to solve the problem of old b
ir facades to the new air-conditioned boxes of space w

Hydraulic Station, Technical University, West Berlin, '
-up bathroom trap. The tradition of *architecture parlan*
and one underlined by colour. (Peter Cook)

11 SEI'CHI SHIRAI, *Noa Building*, Tokyo, 1973-5. Juxtaposition of black offices and brick showroom, white lettering and mordant black, overscaled Renaissance archway and lumpy, cylindrical base. All these contrasts are increased by the typical Shirai aesthetic of minimal articulation and stripped surface.

12 FERDINAND CHEVAL, *Palais Idéal*, Hautrives, 1879-1912. The agglomeration of pebbles collected by this French postman to construct his ideal, miniature world which juxtaposes grottoes and palm trees, galleries and fruits, cascades and animals and a plethora of stylistic quotes from Baroque, Buddhist, and Indian architecture. The idea of a miniaturized world, a *spectaculum mundi*, recurs in backyard gardens and naive, folk architecture. (Architectural Association)

13 FERDINAND CHEVAL, *Palais idéal,* giants gallery, with beasts and diminutive women in Cretan dress. 'One day I stubbed my toe on a stone and almost fell. The offending stone was of such an unusual shape that I picked it up and took it with me. Seeing that nature displays itself as a sculpture, I said to myself, I shall become a mason and an architect'. The palace is eighty-five feet wide, twenty-six feet deep, and thirty-three feet high. Cheval spent two years building the cascade, four on the Druids' Tomb and seven on the Pharaoh's mausoleum. (Architectural Association)

4 SIMON RODIA, *Tower of Watts,* Watts, Los Angeles, 1921-54. Towers of various size (a small one can be seen in the back ground) were built up from metal skeletons covered with cement and decorated with broken plates, glass and shells. Rodia an Italian immigrant who worked as a tile setter, built this monument in gratitude to his host community. He saw it as ship of salvation, but the result, like Cheval's, is a mixed metaphor recalling Gothic spires, spider's webs, Western oil rigs Christmas trees, Towers of Babel, fireworks and an imaginary landscape of slender peaks and honeycombed caves.

5 JAMES WINES and S.I.T.E., *Notch Project*, Sacramento, California, 1976-77. Every morning at 9.00 a.m. this front oor slides open for shoppers, but unlike other push-button apertures it takes part of the building with it, forty-five tons o gged-edged engineering brick. The handling of the 'ripped joint' is carefully realistic; it follows the angle of shear which ight occur in an earth quake, and a few bricks are missing near the points of violence. This is the third of SITE's projects

6 JAMES WINES and S.I.T.E., *Indeterminate Facade*, Houston, Texas, 1974-5. An advertisement which trumps the gloss structures of the Houston strip by turning the dumb box into a construction (or demolition) site. Wines' jokes are met physically inspired, the crumble here shows the simultaneous existence of entropy and order. The public fascination wi disaster and ruins is also a motive. The extreme contrast of BEST and 'worst' is no doubt also intended. (S.I.T.E.)

17 LUCIEN KROLL and ATELIER, *Medical Faculty Buildings*, University of Louvain, near Brussels, 1969-74. Here 'the crumble' climbs up the side of the wall becoming not only an 'earthslide', but also the 'root' of a tree: it's one that branches out in different materials including asbestos tile, concrete block and two kinds of brick. The shaping of masonry so that it runs over two surfaces set at right angles to each other (wall and floor) recalls Antonio Gaudí's experiments.

18 BRUCE GOFF, *Joe Price House,* Bartlesville, Oklahoma, 1956-. Goff belongs in the Pantheon of Bizarre architects along with Borromini and Gaudi. He, like they, uses various geometries and materials in a way which is spatial, structural and metaphorical all at once. Here triangular and hexagonal shapes explode into copper roofs, a sun-screen of white stars, green-blue crystal and strange yellow spikes. Note how the T.V. and rooster feel at home here. (Bruce Goff)

19 BRUCE GOFF, *Price House interior addition*, 1976 +. Creamy, viscuous surfaces slide toward the light and break up into glistening mirrored triangles and another explosion — of protoplasmic ooze, buttons, sequins, plastic, marbles, and golden copper wedges. Actually this loft with its built-in onyx desk and cabinets is a luxurious entertainment area with multi-track stereo and projection equipment which can give as many hallucinatory effects as the architecture. (Bruce Goff)

20 *Sausalito Bay Boat Houses*, California, 1960-. Like the Handmade Homes of California, these self-built, wooden structures incorporate all possible sources and whims. Here a High-Styled Venturi slums next to a Bay Area Rustic. The wit of juxtaposition is often unintentional, but clearly the odd shapes — that diminutive black arcade — are intended.

21 *Sausalito Seaside-Vernacular next to Real Boat and Fifties-Caravan*. Most of these boats move no more than ‘mobile homes; personalisation reaches its ultimate in a community with no aesthetic control; the intermediate technology of buzz saw, hammer and nails can create an architecture as responsive as painting or clothing.

22 SID GRAUMAN, *Chinese Theatre,* Hollywood, 1927 (Meyer and Holler architects). Late-Ming style *porte-cochère* fo
movie stars and their hand prints preserved in concrete. The thin spikey finials and Rococo swoops were obviously influence
by graphic art and the whole idea of a bouquet; this was the traditional place for world premieres.

23 CHARLES Z. KLAUDER, *Cathedral of Learning*, Pittsburgh, 1926-37. Forty storeys of limestone in the Too-Late-Perpendicular style make this the last great monument to collegiate Gothic. The idea of the complete modern university existing within a Monastic enclosure is logical as well as bizarre, and here the heaven-soaring pile provides a marvellous navigation point to the surrounding city, much more comforting than the usual communications tower.

4 A. ALABYAN, *Red Army Theatre*, Moscow 1935-40. In plan a five pointed star symbol of the Red Army — somethin
hat Kruschev derided in 1961 as a formalism only perceivable from the air. Stairs and dressing rooms are placed in the points

5 UNNAMED, *Moscow State University*, Lenin Hills, Moscow, 1947-53? One can navigate around Moscow because of th
everal massive skyscrapers finished in the Stalinist Baroque style. The centralisation and tight-packing in this universit
uilding are as excessive as in any Modern, Western equivalent. With unintended irony, Czarist symbolism of oppression, th

6 M. WELLS and CLEMENS, *Uniroyal Tire Factory*, (originally Samson Rubber Company) Los Angeles, 1929. Th
ssyrian walls and decorations were chosen because they 'symbolized the strength and quality of tires'. The figure of Kin
imroud-Calech holds a staff, and Winged Genii pollinate a sacred tree.

27 *Belvedere Hotel*, Melbourne, Australia, c. 1970. A drive-in Moorish-Gothic Castle one brick deep with its perfectly regula crennelations and gun-slit windows. The heraldic neon sign, a white charger and its flag, move at night. The combinatio of modern technology and ancient imagery produces an hallucination which is not displeasing. Modern architecture wa never this flat. Note the expansion joints.

TYPEWRITERS
CARNITAS y MENUDO
MEXICAN FOOD
AUTHENTIC Mexican Food MENUDO SAT. & SU

29 *Hotel Megaro Emperor,* Tokyo, 1973. One of many eclectic love-hotels which contains romantic suites in differen styles. Bizarre architecture used as an aphrodisiac. Note the way two styles are cleverly interwoven: Ludwig II, or Disney land-castellated, is merged with Age of Plastic, the curved corners and round windows.

0 ARATA ISOZAKI, *RK and RM Robots*, Expo 70, Osaka, 1970. Under the giant space frame, itself a technologica
antasy designed by Kenzo Tange, were these chunky metallic cubes which puttered around with their bug-eyes and flexin
entacles as good robots do. The Technobsession with round lights, funnels, tubes, joints and slick surfaces. Note Isozaki
ed travelling boom of lights above. In retrospect all of these forms look very architectural, even classical. (Dennis Crompton

31 WILLI WALTER, *Swiss Pavilion*, Expo 70, Osaka, 1970. At night this giant, stylised tree lit up with a million bulb urned into a kind of electric Mondrian (who probably influenced the design in any case). World Fairs have fed Technologica ... partly because they are in the business of selling it. The idea that Switzerland is an electric Christmas Tree is nice t

32 YOJI WATANABE, *New Sky Building No. 3.*, Tokyo, 1967-71. Five banks of apartments reach out to the light and view. The image of stacked Airstream bodies, (real) air-conditioning units and at the top a ship's deck. Traditional tea-rooms are placed behind the furthest Airstream bodies. Actually the building uses traditional constructional methods, not the plug

33 YOJI WATANABE, *New Sky Building No. 5*, Tokyo, 1971. 'Exhaust pipes for dragging down the street' deck this concrete apartment tower that was originally conceived as an aluminium space-probe (or upside-down rooster as some Japanese said). Weird effects are achieved by the slight curves which visually dislodge the balconies. The curves and face relate it to Animalorphic Architecture (44-60).

34 RICHARD ROGERS and RENZO PIANO, *Pompidou Centre*, Paris, 1977. Gigantic trusses made by Krupp a through the streets of Paris before the traffic crush. The meccano-set fantasy with the emphasis on the 'Gerb pin joints and spikey, insect-like members is very reminiscent of the Art Nouveau fascination with mechanomorphi

am, c. 1972. An *adhoc* juxtaposition of a jet body and

ingbridge, Hampshire, c. 1972. Thatch and half-timbere

37 ANON, *Baptist Churchmobile*, Brannockstown, Co. Kildare, Ireland, c. 1972. Instead of the drive-in Church, whic
Richard Neutra and Philip Johnson have designed, there is the drive-away church in Gothic, blue-stone aluminium. (Kevi

38 FRANK LLOYD WRIGHT, *Beth Shalom Synagogue*, Elkins Park, Pennsylvania, 1956. A massive substructure with it prow-like corners carries the hexagonal boat of glass which soars up to little Indian finials which repeat the geometrical motif of the whole building. (John Ross, Architectural Association)

39 MICHAEL GRAVES, *Schulman House,* Princeton, New Jersey, 1976. Eclectic fragments from the past are geometriciz
n this addition to a clapboard house. The hieratic, stepped ziggurat is used for doorway and chimney, a rusticated base
mplied by the green (ground) paint while the blue obviously signifies the sky. Note the way 'frontality' is imposed by t
... as well as the diminution in clapboard size. The keystone is a very bizarre mixture of ground and sky.

) PAOLO PORTOGHESI, *Casa Papanice*, Rome, 1969-70. Geometrical themes of circles and semi-curves recur in all par
f this apartment, especially in the roof which has an explosion of organ-pipe cylinders. The building was 'composed accordin
) variations on a Vivaldi', with light blue tiles curving down from the sky, and earth colours rising up from the ground. Th

41 PAOLO PORTOGHESI, *Casa Papanice interior* plays the coloured stripes and curves horizontally to wrap around walls and even curtains, sending the room into high torque. Ripples of white discs fall down from the ceiling to mark important areas for seating, fire or dining. The various window conditions, and views, are also marked with these discs and mirrors. (Paolo Portoghesi)

42 PETER EISENMAN, *House III* for Robert Miller, Lakesville, 1971. A well-designed collision of two right-angled geometrie at 45° which is worked through all parts of the building on an homogeneous, white surface. Because normally distinguishe elements, such as column, roof and wall, are given the same treatment the effect of architecture suspending its normal law is even greater. (Peter Eisenman)

43 PETER EISENMAN, *House III*, interior collisions. Note the care with which elements slide past or abut each other. The overall rectalinear grid is kept in constant view so that variations from it are easily perceived. The building is so abstract in some areas that it could be turned upside-down and there would be no difference. (Peter Eisenman)

ANIMALORPHIC (EXPRESSIONISM)

44 ERICH MENDELSOHN, *Einstein Tower*, Potsdam, 1917-21. Light from the stars is taken through the telescope in th dome and bent downwards to the laboratory, which is maintained at a constant temperature in its heavy basement. Th flowing lines starting at the entrance arms gather force in the convex neck to be fully stopped in the head of the sphinx which seems ready to spring. This animalorphic building follows the logic of the body in treating orifices surrounded b folds and eyelids. (Dennis Sharp)

45 HANS SCHAROUN, *Philharmonic Hall foyer*, Berlin, 1950-63. Architecture as frozen music and frozen movement i
expressed in this foyer with cascades of steps, leaning columns and sloping walls. The purely formal delight in white shape
provides as fitting a backdrop to musical performance as a Rococo interior.

46 RUDOLF STEINER and ASSISTANTS, *Second Goetheanum*, Dornach, 1924-8. A commanding horse-shoe crab lif
ts helmet and takes the measure of the approaching visitor. This auditorium for Steiner's Anthroposophical Society is th
ocus of the Colony, and a built demonstration of his cosmic symbolism – 'plastically moulded laws of nature'. The eyelic
nd window treatment are similar to Gaudi's and Mendelsohn's (44,53). (Peter Blundell Jones)

47 RUDOLF STEINER with ALFRED HILLIGER, *Boilerhouse*, Dornach, 1914-15. Animalorphism at its most lyrical. The rising smoke is symbolised in the stem and buds of a tree, while Steiner's favorite motif, the dome, is doubled to make this also a phallic image, amazing as a mixed conceit. Further plant-like articulations around the windows and the slight suggestion that an animal face is about to push its way out of the wall add to the terror. (Dennis Sharp)

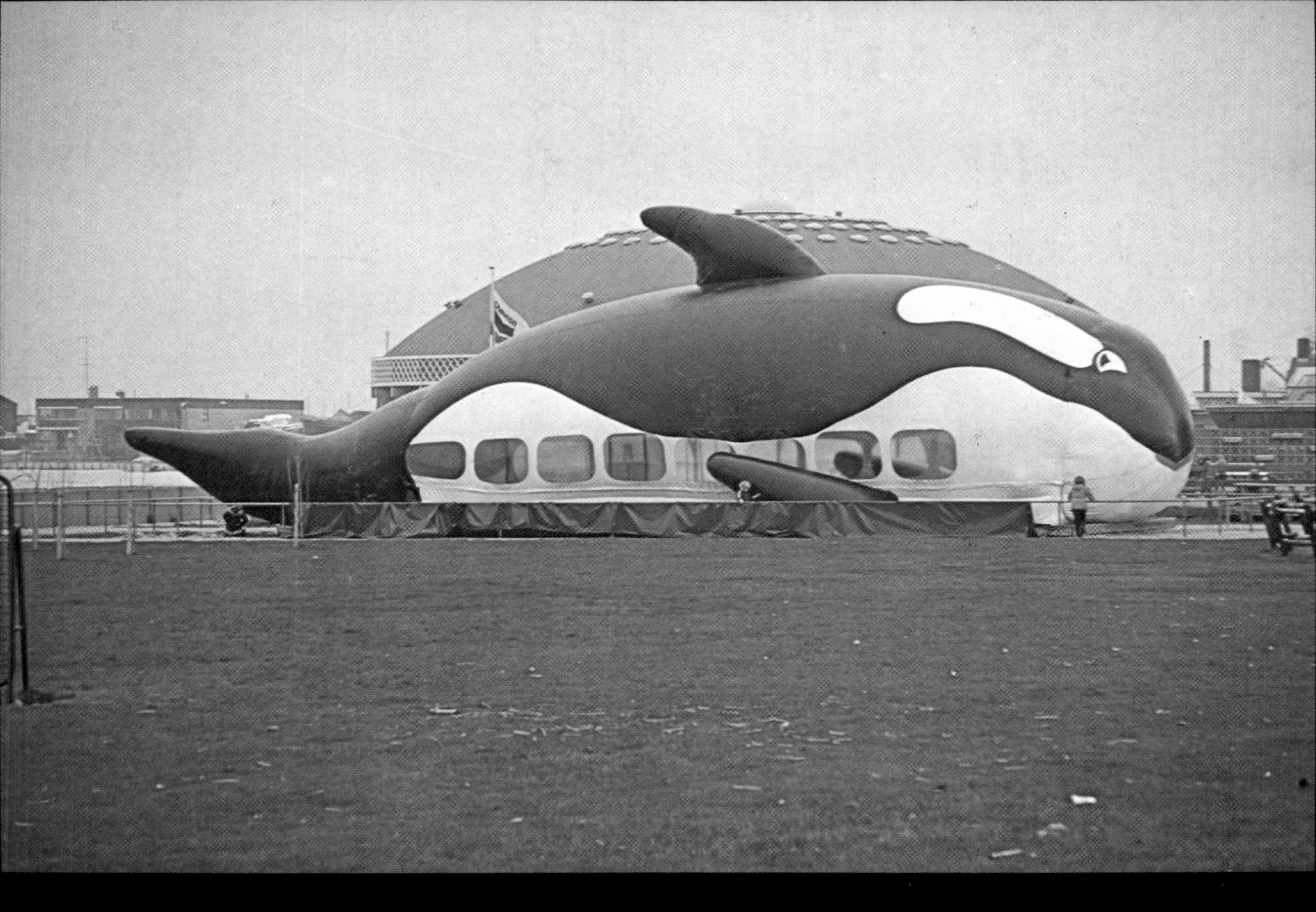

48 ANON, *Inflatable-Whale*, near Eindhoven, Holland, 1975. Pneumatic technology provided many such zoomorphic build-ings for children in the sixties. Among the strange effects they changed the sound and feeling of space, becoming much more tactile and organic than 'hard' architecture.

9 EERO SAARINEN, *Ingalls Hockey Rink,* New Haven, 1957. This whale at Yale undulates its dorsal fin and, under it lack jet nose, opens a big grin for the 3,000 spectators to enter. The slight catenary curves and S-curves are carefull alanced in a Baroque manner. This building launched Yale's patronage of Modern Architecture in its Late phase.

50 *Dinosaur-Dinosaur,* Los Angeles, c. 1974. A favourite entrance to architectural mastodons is through the tail. This lizar which sells curios and old bones, looks as if it had just walked out of the hills in deep focus. Californians have been maki fantasy films for so long that their life begins to imitate their art. (Environmental Communications)

51 JORN UTZON, *Sydney Opera House*, Australia, 1957-74. A mixed animalorphic architecture with a metaphor fo everyone: fish swallowing each other, a traffic accident – no survivors, shells on the beach, sails in the harbour, petals ur folding in growth, and a scrum of nuns.

OLBRICH, *Face House* ('Haus Glückert'), Darmstadt, 1905. This building with its three eyes and ci
embles Face homes in the 'Wee Willie Winkle' cartoons of the time. Olbrich was a master at contrasti
d with plain surface, curve with rectangle and one style with another (see also 3).

53 ANTONIO GAUDI, *Casa Milá Roofscape*, Barcelona, 1905-10. Animalorphic forms, including the parabola, frame Gaudi's ultimate building, the Sagrada Familia Church. Chimney hoods become an excuse for creating a race of helmeted warriors which exist in groups, or as here, singularly. Exit stairs become rather fatter and more lovable giants. (Carol Shields, Architectural Association)

54 RUDOLF STEINER, *Studio Building* ('Glashaus'), Dornach, 1913-14. This workshop clad in a hide of wooden shingles has a door within a door that looks out at you with amusement and sadness. The contrast of colors and materials, the ornament stemming from the nature of the material, were typical ideas of Steiner. (see also 46,47). (Mark Richardson, Architectural Association)

55 *Beware of the Dog Face House*, Somewhere in California, c. 1965? Perhaps the sign should read 'Beware of the House
The mouth is definitely open, the nose tightly closed and the eyes squinting, just before the bite. (John Beach)

56 ROBERT VENTURI and JOHN RAUCH, *Brant-Johnson House*, Vail, Colorado, 1976. A ski vacation house with space at the top of the tower oriented to the fireplace. The face image is combined with traditional eave and curved window that are exaggerated to give a toy-like scale. Note the change of direction in the siding, which according to bizarre Venturi usage, occurs in the middle of windows rather than floors. (Robert Venturi)

-House', San Francisco, c. 1960? This was so named
upper left window). The symmetrical facade often is im
nce, a house morphology shares several features with the

Facade, London Exhibition on Post-Modernism, 1977.
buldings, was meant to imitate a bust of Sir Edwin Lu

59 C. A. JENCKS, *Bay Window Face*, Studio, Cape Cod, 1977. The plastic eyes can just be seen behind the cu
the teeth and hair are hard to make out from this view; various planes were picked out in four different

ANIMALORPHIC (FACE HOUSES)

60 BRUCE GOFF, *Gryder House*, Ocean Springs, Mississippi, 1959-60. This Chinese ant-eater squints up its eyes, bristles its comb and sends out its snozzle across the lily-pond garden to suck up the unwary visitor. The Gryders like the way the colors of the building fit in with the pine forest. Goff is as conscious about making faces as Gaudi was. Note the unbelievable conic balconies. (B. M. Boyle)

61 ANON, *Deschwanden's Shoe Repairs*, Bakersfield, California, c. 1951. The Shoe has been a house at least since 'there was an old woman'. But never a white buck, with elevated platform. The architect hasn't quite solved the problem of entry and view. Should the sign read 'Empty'? (John Beach)

62 ANON, *Big Donut Drive-In*, Los Angeles, c. 1954. There used to be ten of these giant donuts, now there are only three left. Sugary-brown, twenty feet tall and made out of plaster, the thing might appear as a lost 747 wheel without the written sign.

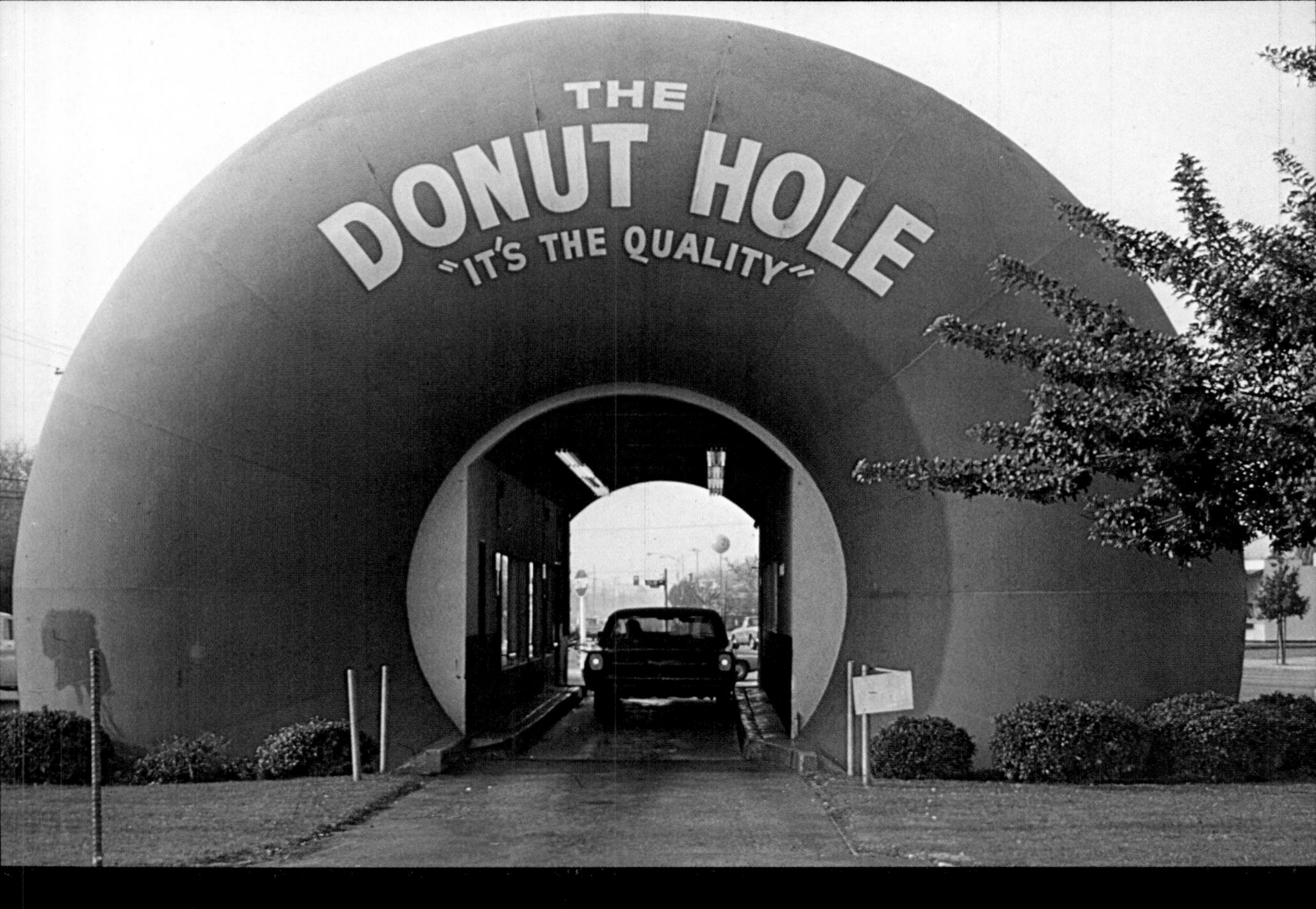

63 ANON, *The Donut Hole*, La Puente, California, c. 1963. Again without the written sign the neighbours might have thought it was something *much* worse than a donut. As far as I know the car wash doesn't serve donuts; 'it's the quality' of the water or the hole, perhaps. (John Beach)

64 ROBERT VENTURI and JOHN RAUCH, *Dixwell Fire Station*, New Haven, 1970-73. A simple brick box where th brick peels out at the corner, and hangs, to 'accommodate' the lettering. Venturi has used the conventions of the civi building and billboard to produce this bizarre dumb box, and he has constructed a long, dumb poem ('Rescue Truck Co. Engine Co. 6 Engine Co. 3') to justify the hanging brick. Note the half-rustication, the white brick, and token use of marbl by the entrance.